Campbell's
CONDENSED
MINESTRONE
SOUP

Campbell's
CONDENSED
CREAM OF VEGETABLE
SOUP

Campbell's
CONDENSED
TURKEY
NOODLE
SOUP

Campbell's
CONDENSED
PEPPER POT
SOUP

Campbell's
CONDENSED
CONSOMMÉ
(BEEF)
SOUP

Campbell's
CONDENSED
CLAM CHOWDER
SOUP

Campbell's
CONDENSED

Campbell's
CONDENSED
BEEF BROTH
(BOUILLON)
SOUP
Campbell's
CONDENSED
BEEF
SOUP

Campbell's
CONDENSED
CREAM OF
ASPARAGUS
SOUP

VEGETABLE

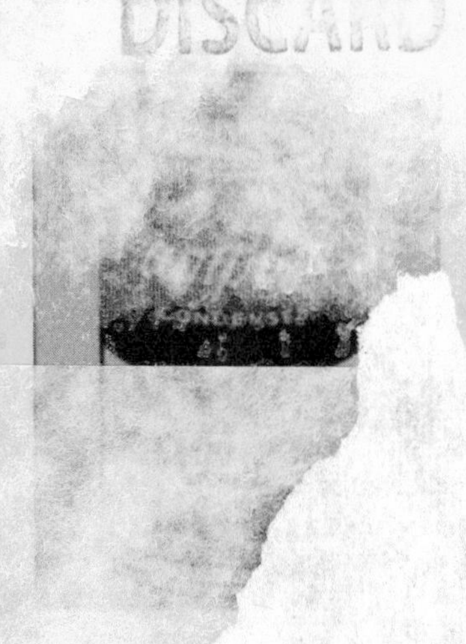

Campbell's
CONDENSED
VEGETABLE
BEAN
SOUP

Campbell's
CONDENSED
CREAM OF
CELERY
SOUP

Campbell's
CONDENSED
CHICKEN
GUMBO
SOUP

BEAN

Campbell's
CONDENSED
VEGETABLE
SOUP

Campbell's
CONDENSED
TOMATO
SOUP

Endpapers: *Campbell's Soup Cans,*
by Andy Warhol, 1961–1962, oil on
canvas, Collection of Irving Blum,
courtesy Leo Castelli Gallery, New York

Study: Falling Man (Wheel Man)
1965, by Ernest Trova
silicon bronze, Collection
Walker Art Center, Minneapolis
courtesy The Pace Gallery, New York

The Art of America Since World War II

By Shirley Glubok

Designed by Gerard Nook

MACMILLAN PUBLISHING CO., INC.
New York
COLLIER MACMILLAN PUBLISHERS
London

The author gratefully acknowledges the kind assistance of:
Karen and *Cheryl Nook; Vivvie* and *Suzanne Le Corbeiller;*
and especially the helpful cooperation of
HENRY GELDZAHLER, Curator,
Twentieth Century Art, The Metropolitan Museum of Art

Other books by Shirley Glubok:

THE ART OF ANCIENT EGYPT
THE ART OF LANDS IN THE BIBLE
THE ART OF ANCIENT GREECE
THE ART OF THE NORTH AMERICAN INDIAN
THE ART OF THE ESKIMO
THE ART OF ANCIENT ROME
THE ART OF AFRICA
ART AND ARCHAEOLOGY
THE ART OF ANCIENT PERU
THE ART OF THE ETRUSCANS
THE ART OF ANCIENT MEXICO
KNIGHTS IN ARMOR
THE ART OF INDIA
THE ART OF JAPAN
THE ART OF COLONIAL AMERICA
THE ART OF THE SOUTHWEST INDIANS
THE ART OF THE OLD WEST
THE ART OF THE NEW AMERICAN NATION
THE ART OF THE SPANISH IN THE UNITED STATES AND PUERTO RICO
THE ART OF CHINA
THE ART OF AMERICA FROM JACKSON TO LINCOLN
THE ART OF AMERICA IN THE GILDED AGE
THE ART OF AMERICA IN THE EARLY TWENTIETH CENTURY
THE ART OF THE NORTHWEST COAST INDIANS
THE ART OF THE PLAINS INDIANS
THE FALL OF THE AZTECS
THE FALL OF THE INCAS
DISCOVERING TUT-ANKH-AMEN'S TOMB
DISCOVERING THE ROYAL TOMBS AT UR
DIGGING IN ASSYRIA
HOME AND CHILD LIFE IN COLONIAL DAYS
DOLLS, DOLLS, DOLLS

With Alfred Tamarin:

ANCIENT INDIANS OF THE SOUTHWEST
VOYAGING TO CATHAY: AMERICANS IN THE CHINA TRADE

Front cover illustration: *Cinnamon Burn,* by Helen Frankenthaler, 1968, acrylic on canvas, Private Collection, courtesy André Emmerich Gallery, New York.
Back cover illustration: *Untitled,* by Frank Stella, 1974, acrylic on canvas, courtesy Knoedler Contemporary Art, New York, Lawrence Rubin, Director.

Macmillan Publishing Co., Inc., 866 Third Avenue, New York, N.Y. 10022
Collier Macmillan Canada, Ltd.
Printed in the United States of America

1 2 3 4 5 6 7 8 9 10

Library of Congress Cataloging in Publication Data
Glubok, Shirley. The art of America since World War II.
SUMMARY: A survey of American art from 1940 to the present which includes "white writing," action painting, abstract expressionism, op art, pop art, stabiles, and kinetic sculpture.
1. Art, American—Juvenile literature.
2. Art, Modern—20th century—United States—Juvenile literature.
[1. Art, American. 2. Art, Modern—20th century] I. Title.
N6512.G58 709'.73 75-34453 ISBN 0-02-736310-4

Beginning, by Kenneth Noland, 1958, acrylic on canvas, Hirshhorn Museum and Sculpture Garden, Smithsonian Institution

In 1940 Adolf Hitler's Nazi army invaded France and the Germans occupied Paris. For more than a century Paris had been a great international art center, where painters and sculptors from all over the world gathered to study and work. When France was taken over by the Nazis, many brilliant European modern artists moved to America, joining those who had already left Germany after Hitler came to power. Most of them settled in New York, which became the center of the art world. Now Americans went to New York to study, rather than to Paris.

In the early years after the war and during the decades that followed, new ideas were developed in America that spread throughout the world. In no other place, at no other time, did so many changes take place so rapidly in art.

1944, oil on canvas, The Metropolitan Museum of Art, George A. Hearn Fund, 1956

Among the Europeans who settled in New York were artists known as "surrealists," who were interested in ideas about exploring a person's dreams and hidden thoughts. Arshile Gorky was influenced by the surrealists. Instead of copying nature, he permitted his feelings to control his brush. Gorky worked so freely that he let paint drip down the canvas and become part of the picture. In *Water of the Flowery Mill* at left, shapes that represent plant and animal forms seem to float in space. Gorky spent his boyhood in Armenia and moved to America in the 1920's. Many of the symbols in his paintings represent memories from his childhood. A painting that uses forms and symbols to represent objects is called "abstract."

When William Baziotes started on a painting, he did not know what images would appear. Mysterious creatures that haunt strange worlds emerged on his canvases and surprised even the artist himself. *Dragon*, below, has a large head with a wide, open mouth. The creature seems to balance on a sharp point of the simple, flat shape that forms its body.

1950, oil on canvas,
The Metropolitan Museum of Art,
Arthur H. Hearn Fund, 1950

George Tooker painted scenes of places and people that look real, yet the subjects were taken from the inner world of his imagination. *Government Bureau* represents a large city office where people have to wait in lines and talk to workers who might be unpleasant. The room looks like something in a bad dream. The office workers peer through holes and their hands rest on machine keyboards.

1956, egg tempera on gesso panel, The Metropolitan Museum of Art, George A. Hearn Fund, 1

The standing figures of a man and a woman are repeated to make it seem that they have to stand in line a long time. The hanging lamps and pillars and the glass cubicles also are repeated, making the scene all the more frightening.

Many of Richard Lindner's paintings are based on memories of his childhood in Germany. The doll-like figure in *The Child's Dream* is mysteriously suspended in a tiny room furnished with strange playthings. Lindner, who collects toys, was brought up in Nuremberg, a city famous as the toy center of the world. He fled to France in 1933 when the Nazis started to make life difficult for Jewish people in Germany. He settled in America after Hitler took over Paris.

1952, oil on canvas, Whitney Museum of American Art, New York, Gift of Mr. and Mrs. Theodore V. Marsters

Oil on canvas, The St. Louis Art Museum

The make-believe world of children's play attracted Philip Guston when he saw a group of boys fighting an imaginary war. The flat shapes of the boys' bodies, their wide, staring eyes and the blank windows on the buildings in the background add a feeling of mystery. *Martial Memory* was painted in 1941, the year the United States entered World War II. Soon afterward Guston changed his style completely, along with many other leading artists of the period. He no longer paints figures and other subject matter that can be recognized.

Jacob Lawrence paints the real world. His subjects are people on the streets of Harlem, events in the lives of famous Black Americans and men at work. In *Cabinet Makers* the figures of the carpenters are simple shapes, yet the positions of their bodies show how hard they are working.

1946, gouache on paper, Hirshhorn Museum and Sculpture Garden, Smithsonian Institution

ADOLPH GOTTLIEB

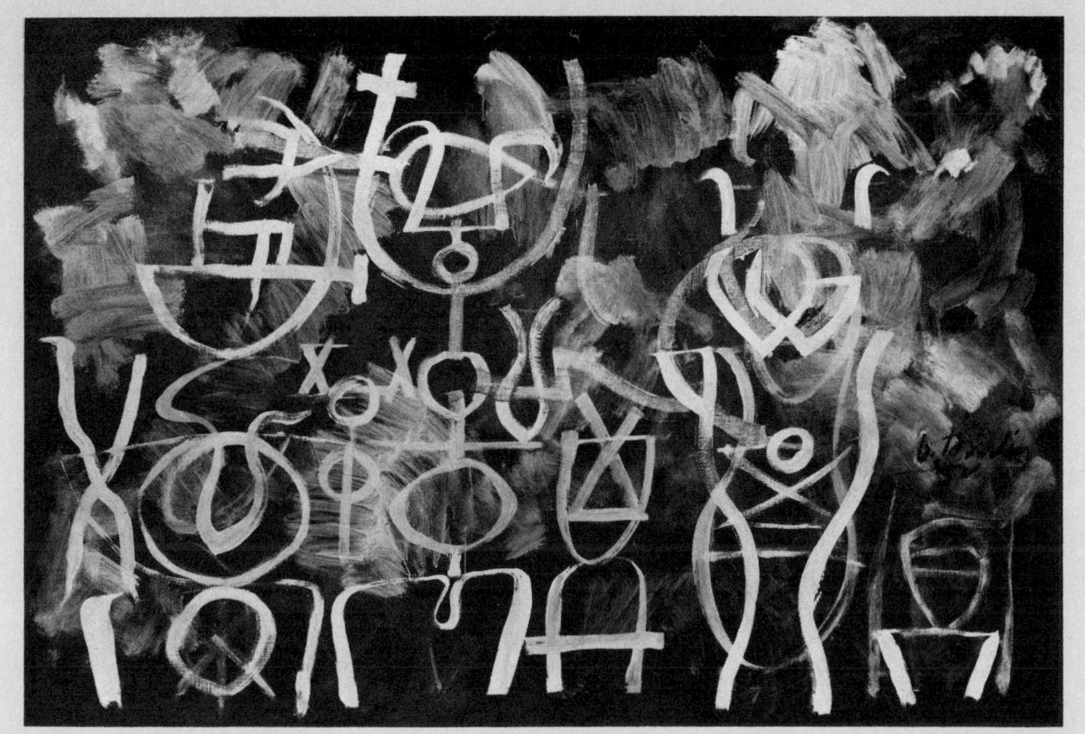

1948, oil on canvas, courtesy Betty Parsons Gallery, New York

While living briefly in Arizona, Adolph Gottlieb would gather specimens of animal life and desert plants and arrange them on a tabletop. Gottlieb would make paintings of these objects, adding forms from prehistoric Indian drawings, ancient mythology and from his own imagination. He painted lines to separate the symbols on his canvas into boxlike compartments. The symbols have no connection with each other, but together they form an interesting pattern. Gottlieb called these paintings "pictographs," and named the one at left *Voyager's Return*.

Bradley Walker Tomlin, who admired Gottlieb's pictographs, traveled in the Far East and studied Chinese calligraphy, or brush writing. His *All Souls Night* is painted loosely with twisting white brush strokes on a dark background. The calligraphic signs are placed freely over the canvas.

)46, oil on canvas,
he Museum of Modern Art,
ew York, Gift of
Ir. and Mrs. Roy R. Neuberger

Mark Tobey also traveled to China and Japan, where he studied calligraphy and became interested in Oriental art. In *Drums, Totems and the Word of God* at right, his white brush strokes form tall totem poles, carved wooden masks and symbols of the Indians of the Northwest Coast, where Tobey lives. At the bottom of the painting, a man in a cloak and hat reads from a large book, probably a prayer book. Tobey is deeply involved in the Bahai faith that teaches the unity of mankind. He also has been interested in Zen Buddhism, a Japanese religion that teaches self-discipline and quiet thinking in order to attain wisdom.

Another Northwest Coast artist who is interested in Zen Buddhism and Oriental art is Morris Graves. He lives a quiet life in the woods, apart from the rest of the world, and has developed his own private style of painting. Graves, who is concerned with the inner meanings of the world, is disturbed by machine-age pollution and noise. Nature is the subject of his work, especially lone birds, which stand for solitude.

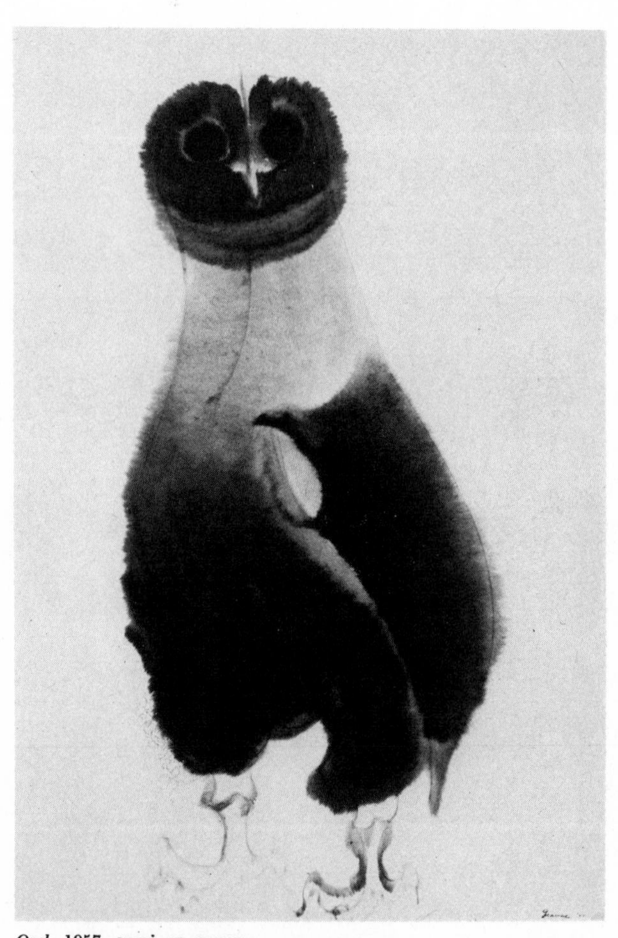

Owl, 1957, sumi on paper,
Collection of Sir Robert Adeane, London,
courtesy Willard Gallery, New York

1944, tempera on boa
Estate of Herman Shulma
courtesy Willard Galle

No images or symbols can be recognized in *Autumn Rhythm* by Jackson Pollock. The act of creating a painting was more important to this artist than the finished work. Instead of using an easel, Pollock would tack a huge sheet of canvas to the wall or spread it on the floor. Then he would walk around it, approaching it from all sides, in order to "get into" the painting. Pollock worked with sticks, trowels, knives and his fingers, as well as with house painter's brushes. He dragged, dripped, dribbled, trickled, poured, spattered and even flung ordinary house paint onto the canvas at high speed, distributing it over the entire surface in wild, swinging streaks and curves.

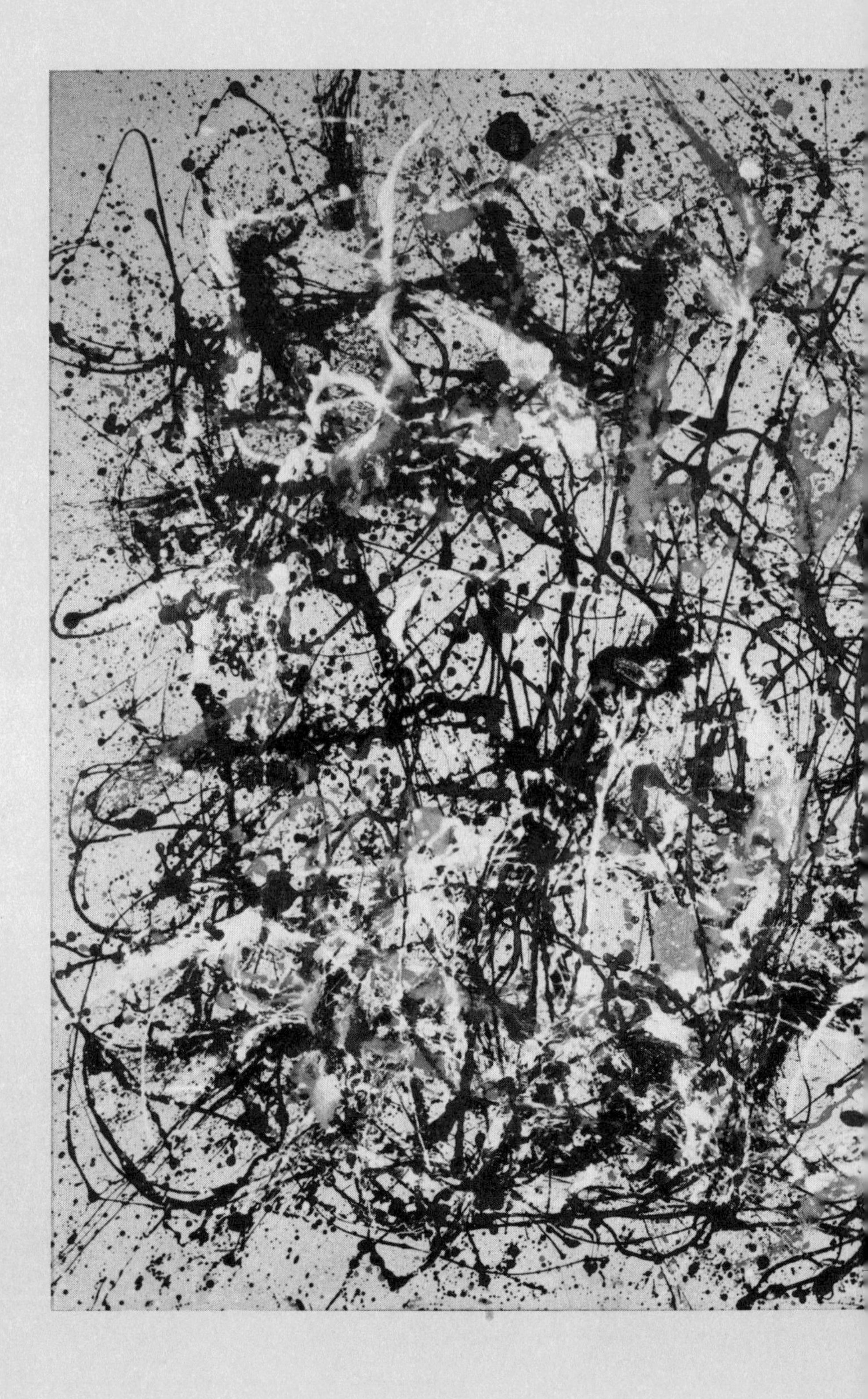

1950, oil on canvas, The Metropolitan Museum of Art, George A. Hearn Fund, 1957

1953–1954, oil on canvas, Albright-Knox Art Gallery, Buffalo, New York, Gift of Seymour H. Knox

Using the motion of the whole body to act out one's feelings on a canvas came to be called "action painting." It is a form of "abstract expressionism," which was the most important art movement in the entire world in the mid-twentieth century.

The abstract expressionist tries to express his own experiences and inner feelings, creating works in which the subject matter cannot be recognized.

Robert Motherwell, who grew up in California, is one of America's important abstract expressionists. In 1936, when he was a young man, the Spanish Civil War broke out. When the Spanish Republic was overthrown, Motherwell felt that a terrible death had occurred that should not be forgotten. Years later he expressed his grief in the picture at left called *Elegy to the Spanish Republic #34*. An elegy is a funeral song. The large black shapes in the painting stand for death; the white in the background stands for life.

Hans Hofmann, a German who settled in New York in the 1930's, was interested in the "cubist" style. Instead of copying the natural shapes of things, the cubists use squares, rectangles, circles, pyramids and cones to represent them. *The Window* is a balanced arrangement of solid forms, composed of straight lines and sharp angles, that seem to move in space. Hofmann became one of America's most important teachers of modern art, and a leading abstract expressionist.

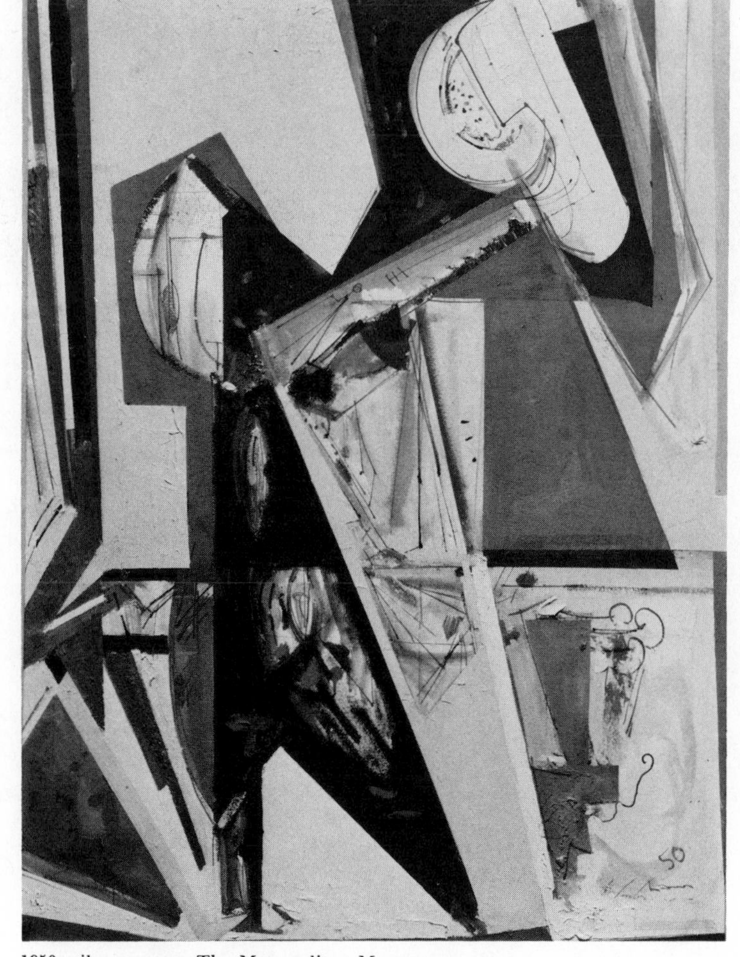

1950, oil on canvas, The Metropolitan Museum of Art, Gift of Mr. and Mrs. Roy R. Neuberger, 1951

1943-1946, oil and charcoal on board, Hirshhorn Museum and Sculpture Garden, Smithsonian Institution

Willem de Kooning worked with cubist ideas when he painted *Queen of Hearts.* The queen's nose, eyes, hair, breasts, arms and the chair she is sitting in are made up of cubist shapes. De Kooning makes drawings, then cuts them apart and puts them together in different combinations. He carries this idea into his paintings, so that the different parts do not always seem to fit together.

De Kooning, who became a leader of the abstract expressionist movement, was one of the first artists in New York to make his studio in an old warehouse or small factory building. Such a studio, known as a loft, could often be rented cheaply. Lofts are larger than rooms in ordinary houses, so artists can work on huge paintings and sculptures. Most abstract expressionist paintings are very large, sometimes as big as the entire wall of an ordinary room.

At a time when most artists around Larry Rivers are working in a purely abstract style, his paintings usually have figures that can be identified, combined with abstract forms. In *The Sitter,* also known as *Birdie's Breakfast,* Rivers painted his mother-in-law, who often "sat," or posed, for him. She is seen twice, seated at a table, and her pet bird is painted twice also, but all of these forms are left incomplete. The table is shown as though we were looking down on it, with plates that are completely rounded.

1956, oil on can
The Metropolitan Mus
of Art, Gi
Hugo Kastor,

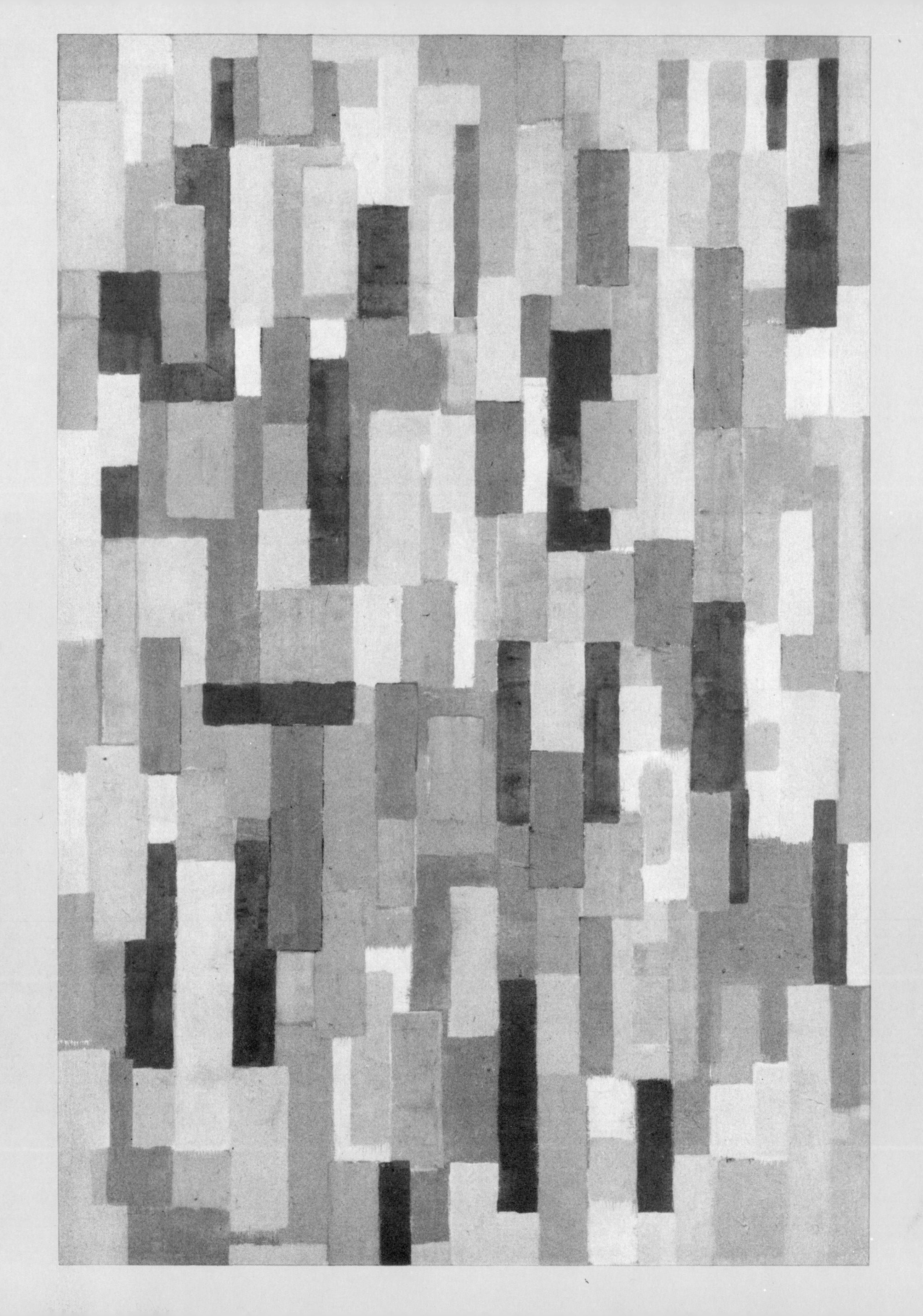

Ad Reinhardt believed that art should represent only itself and not express the painter's inner feelings. He also believed that an artist should have the idea of a painting in his mind before picking up a brush. In *Brick Painting* at left, rectangular bars of paint, almost all of them vertical, cover an entire canvas. Some of the rectangles overlap. They look as if they were cut out and pasted down. To prepare for his paintings, Reinhardt often experimented with collage, cutting out pieces of paper and arranging them on a flat background.

Tight ribbons of color in vertical bands were painted in the middle of a canvas by Morris Louis. Before making a painting, artists usually "size" and "prime" their canvases, covering them with a gluey substance and then with a white coating so the paint will not soak in and the surface will be even. But Louis, using extremely thin paints, poured his colors directly onto the bare canvas, letting them run down in stripes and soak into the cloth, like dye. His works are considered "color field" painting, a form of abstract expressionism in which large areas of color are applied with no suggestion of figures or symbols.

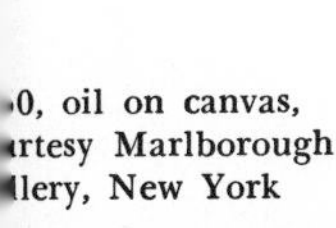
0, oil on canvas,
rtesy Marlborough
llery, New York

Aldebaran, 1962, acrylic on canvas,
courtesy André Emmerich Gallery

Josef Albers uses only four pure colors and one simple shape, placing squares one within the other. He believes in keeping his feelings out of a painting and creating a perfectly simple, orderly picture. Albers was born in Germany. When the Nazis closed the art school where he taught, he moved to America. He taught at Yale University, where Richard Anuszkiewicz was one of his students.

Anuszkiewicz used the square, but turned it on edge and added a series of lines and triangles in his painting at right. The painting seems to be three-dimensional, to have depth, even though it is actually flat. As the light changes and the viewer's eyes shift, it takes on different appearances. Because of its optical effects, relating to the eyes, this style is called "op art."

Homage to the Square: Dedicated, 1955, oil on masonite, Albright-Knox Art Gallery, Gift of the Seymour H. Knox Foundation, Inc.

Primary Center II, 1968, acrylic on board, Private Collection, Indiana, courtesy Sidney Janis Gallery, New York

Subjects for Milton Avery's paintings came from the world around him—his family and friends, the mountains, sea, birds and animals. In *Bucolic Landscape* he enlarged, flattened and simplified the form of a cow into an almost abstract shape. Without unnecessary details, the picture becomes bold and clear.

The paintings of Will Barnet also are simplified. The outlines are so hard and firm that the works look two-dimensional, or flat. Barnet records the private world of his home, catching his family and pets in the midst of daily activities. At right, his daughter concentrates on blowing a soap bubble.

1945, oil on canvas, Albright-Knox Art Gallery, Room of Contemporary Art Fund

The Silent Seasons—Summer, 1967, oil on canvas, Whitney Museum of American Art, Gift of Mr. and Mrs. Daniel H. Silberberg

1961, tempera on board,
Copyright © Andrew Wyeth,
Collection of
Mrs. Norman B. Woolworth

Day Remembered, tempera and casein on masonite, Hirshhorn Museum and Sculpture Garden, Smithsonian Institution

Simple scenes of life in rural America are carefully recorded by Andrew Wyeth. He lives in the country, in Pennsylvania in winter months and Maine in the summer. Wyeth likes to paint outdoors near his homes. In *Distant Thunder* the artist's wife has fallen asleep in the grass after picking berries. Rattler, their dog, has been startled by the sound of thunder. Wyeth's style has not been affected by the drastic changes taking place in the art world. He continues to paint in a realistic manner, recording every berry, flower and blade of grass in great detail.

The small town in Arkansas where Carroll Cloar grew up and fished and wandered barefoot through the woods is the subject of his paintings. Cloar often works from faded snapshots, taken at family gatherings, to recall boyhood memories.

An old snapshot gave Robert Indiana the idea for *Father,* which is painted in a broad, flat style. The painter's father traveled from one end of America to the other in his Model-T Ford. He considered himself strong and hardy, and he was always well dressed, so he is shown barefoot but wearing a high starched collar, overcoat and hat. The father's last name was Clarke, but Robert changed his own name to Indiana, after the state where he was born.

It is common for Indiana, who worked as a sign painter, to use words on his

Detail of *Mother and Father,* 1963–1967, oil on canvas, Collection of the artist

1958, Collection of Mr. and Mrs. Burton Tremaine, Meriden, Connecticut, courtesy Leo Castelli Gallery

pictures and sculptures. He often makes paintings from words alone, as in *Love*, which was used as a design for a United States postage stamp.

The American flag, because it is familiar to every American, was chosen as the subject of *Three Flags* by Jasper Johns. He covered the entire area of a canvas with the flag form, then repeated it on two smaller canvases and attached one on top of the other. *Three Flags* was painted with encaustic, or hot wax colors, which flow easily, do not sink into the canvas, and dry almost instantly.

1966, oil on canvas, Contemporary Art Museum, Nagaoka, Japan, courtesy Leo Castelli Gallery

James Rosenquist earned a living as a painter of enormous billboards. This experience carried over into his paintings, which are often huge, with images that are direct and strong. In *Growth Plan,* above, he places familiar figures in strange arrangements. Rosenquist is one of America's leading "pop artists," a term for those who use subjects from our popular culture.

Roy Lichtenstein got the idea for *Girl with Ball* from a picture he saw advertising a vacation resort. He enlarged the figure of the girl and painted spots on her face and body to look like the tiny dots that can be seen on printed pictures when they are viewed through a magnifying glass. Lichtenstein is known for his paintings of comic strip characters; he has even made drawings from bubble gum wrappers. The pop artist's attachment to the world around him is opposite from the abstract expressionist's concern with his own inner feelings.

1961, oil on canvas,
Private Collection,
courtesy Leo Castelli Gallery

When pop art was introduced in the early 1960's, people were shocked to see ordinary, everyday things used as the subjects of art. Pop artists were particularly interested in showing products sold through the television and radio commercials and magazine and newspaper advertisements that are so much a part of American life. Tom Wesselmann used the door of a real refrigerator and a real picture in a frame in his *Still Life #34*, below. The bottles of soda are plastic display models, and the foods on the table are cut-out pictures from advertisements. Actual artificial

Still Life #30, 1963, Museum of Modern Art, Gift of Philip Johnson

1967, oil on wood, Collection of the artist

flowers sit on the window sill. The curtains are painted by the artist but look stiff, and even the view through the window looks like an advertising picture rather than a natural landscape.

In Maxwell Hendler's *Afternoon Television*, everything is painted to look real. The backs of houses seen through the windows, the window shades, floorboards, books, piano keys and even the picture on the television screen are all painted realistically in the greatest detail. Hendler, who lives in California, works very slowly and carefully on his pictures, which are small and delicate, yet strong.

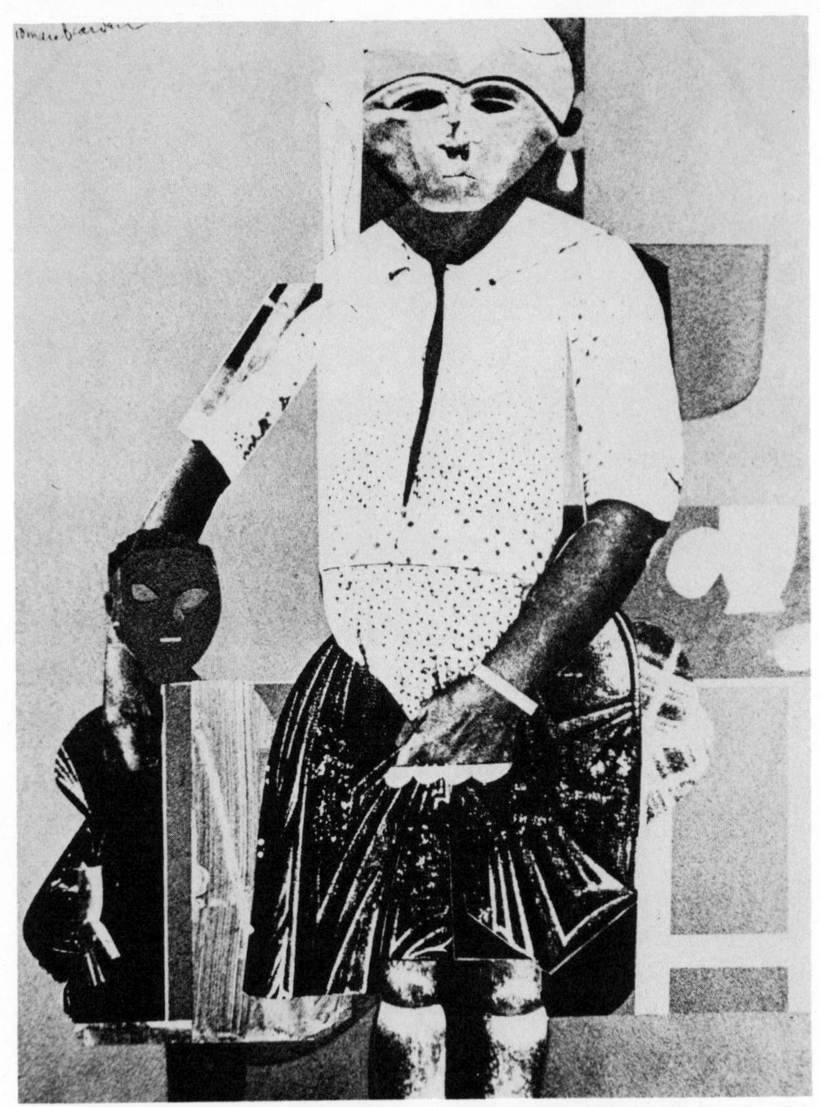

1968, formerly in the Collection of Nanette Rohan Beardon

Romare Beardon uses his own memories and childhood experiences to express the folklore of the rural South and Northern slums in his collages. He cuts out and tears pictures from newspapers and magazines, pieces of colored paper or paper that he has painted, and glues them to the surface in startling combinations. The head of the woman in *Mother and Child* represents an African mask, a reminder of the African origins of Black Americans. Beardon, in addition to being a painter, has written many songs and is co-author of books on art.

An automobile tire encircles a stuffed ram in Robert Rauschenberg's *Monogram*. The goat stands on a flat surface, to which are attached pieces of wood, bits of signs, the heel of a shoe, footprints, cut-out pictures and a pair of shorts. Rauschenberg applied thick paint over the objects, including the face of the goat. He calls this work, which is a combination of painting, collage and construction, a "combine." Rauschenberg's combines are made out of used objects from the real world.

1959, National Museum, Stockholm, Sweden

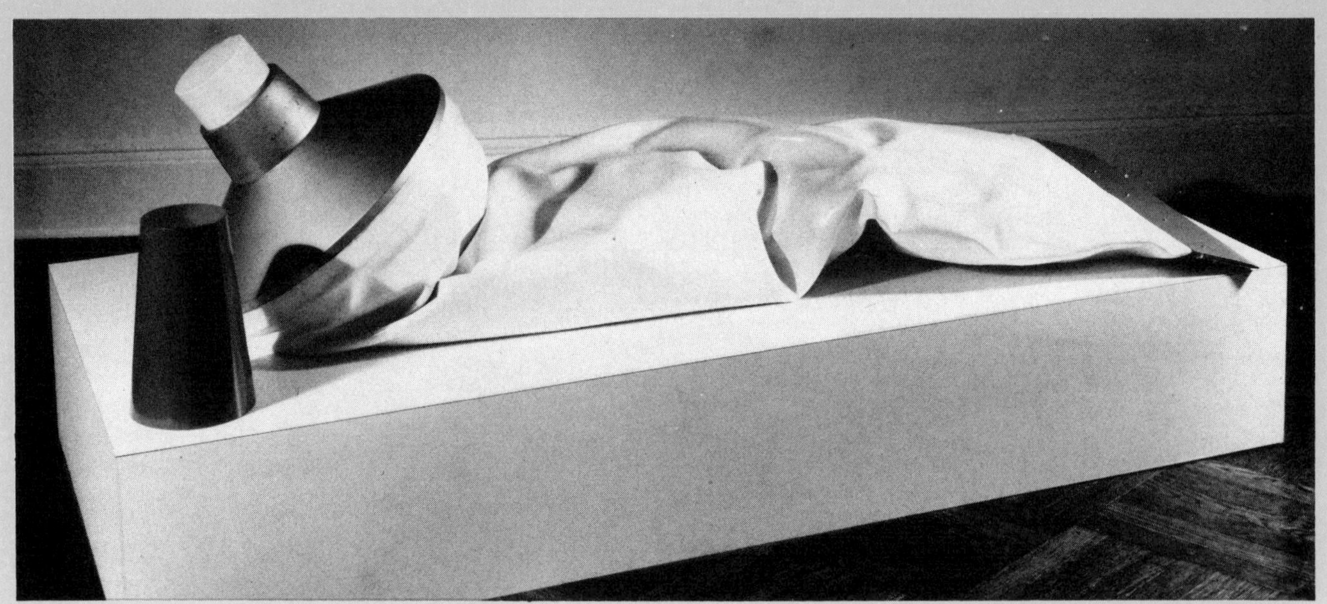

1964, Private Collection, courtesy Leo Castelli Gallery

Items that we use often, especially those that symbolize America, such as hamburgers, hot dogs and ice-cream cones, are made into large three-dimensional objects by Claes Oldenberg. Canvas and a shiny plastic cloth called vinyl are sewn into the shape of the object and stuffed with kapok, a soft fluffy material used for pillows. This giant tube of toothpaste is five and a half feet long; the cap is off and the toothpaste appears to be oozing out.

To make his sculptured works of American scenes all the more real, George Segal makes plaster replicas of people and presents them in their everyday environment, or complete setting. Using his friends as models, he freezes them in position by actually casting them in plaster. He dips strips of cloth in wet plaster and wraps them around the person. When the plaster hardens it is removed in sections, which are later joined together. Segal's life-size, hollow figures are usually left in the natural white of the plaster. In *The Subway* he used part of a discarded subway car as the environment.

1968, Collection
Mrs. Robert B. Ma
Chicago, cour
Sidney Janis Gall

1962, oil on wood, Collection of Mr. and Mrs. Myron Orlofsky, courtesy Sonnabend Gallery, New York

Jim Dine uses actual things from his home, studio or backyard, such as shoes, suits, ties or a lawn mower, to create surprising "assemblages." An assemblage is a work in which three-dimensional objects are attached to a background. In *Black*

Garden Tools, rakes and shovels take on an unusual importance when painted over and hung as a work of art.

From childhood Joseph Cornell loved to save old pictures. He also collected and carefully stored away clock springs, corks, feathers, marbles and jacks. He arranged his pictures and treasures in little shadow boxes with glass windows. For *Medici Princess* at right, Cornell pasted a reproduction of a famous painting by Bronzini, a sixteenth-century Italian artist, inside a box. Then he put smaller copies of the same painting in two vertical rows on either side. He covered different parts of the pictures to create an unexpected pattern. The same picture was even pasted on a block at the lower right and can be seen reflected in a mirror.

About 1952, courtesy
ACA Galleries, Inc., New York

1945, Whitney Museum of American Art

The favorite materials of sculptor David Smith were iron and steel, which he felt were connected with power and progress. Smith worked in an automobile factory when he was young and then in a defense plant during World War II. He assembled metal parts, and learned to cut and bend steel and to use a welding torch to join pieces of metal together. In *Cockfight, Variation* Smith cut out pieces of steel and arranged them to form a composition of birds. Some of the steel pieces were welded together, connected by melted metal; others were riveted, joined together with bolts. Smith's studio was a fully equipped machine shop.

He and Alexander Calder were among the first American sculptors to use new methods and industrial materials for their work. Calder, who invented the mobile, or sculpture that moves, also created the stabile, standing sculpture made of sheet metal that is cut out and then riveted or welded together. Calder makes tiny models for his stabiles by hand, then sends them to an iron works to be enlarged into huge outdoor constructions. *Large Spiny* is twelve and a half feet high.

1966, painted ste
Collection
Nelson A. Rockefell
photograph by Charles U

For her constructions Lee Bontecou collects old canvas laundry bags. She makes a frame by welding together sections of steel, then stretches the canvas over it. The cloth is attached to the frame with copper wire. The hole in the center of the construction adds to the feeling of depth. The work below has no title. Bontecou

1960, Collection of Nelson A. Rockefeller, photograph by Charles Uht

hopes that the audience viewing her works will see and feel whatever they wish.

Isamu Noguchi has worked with many different materials during his long lifetime. Now he prefers stainless steel for large works. To test his ideas, Noguchi cuts and folds paper. Then he transfers his designs onto sheets of steel which he cuts and joins together so skillfully that they, too, appear folded. Finally he polishes the steel with an electric grinder into a textured surface that reflects the light. Steel is tough and hard to work with, but it is long-lasting, so the sculptures can stand in the open air. Artists of today like to make outdoor public sculpture that can be seen by the largest possible audience.

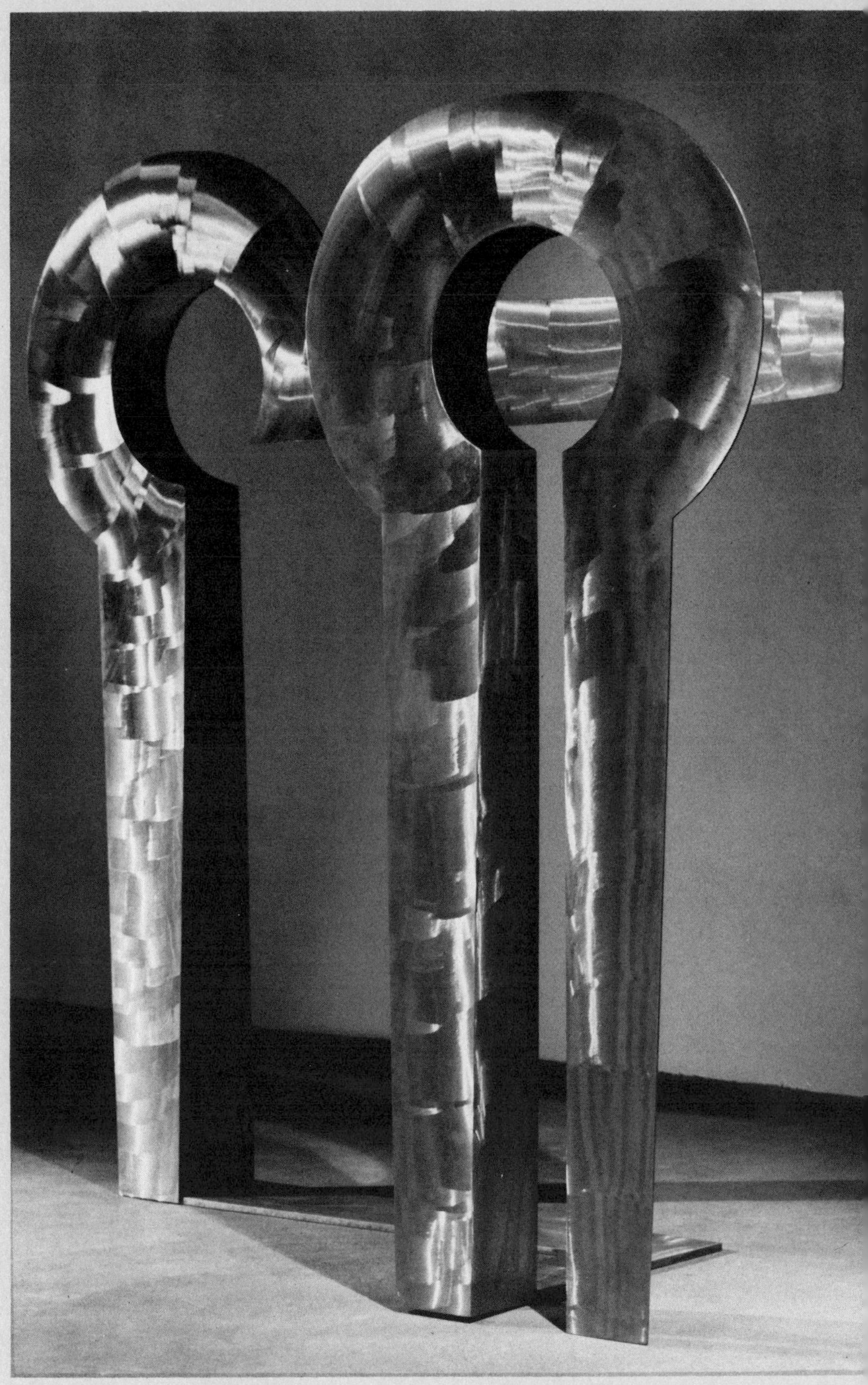

Sentinel, 1973, courtesy The Pace Gallery

Mi Mamá y Yo, 1968,
courtesy Sidney Janis Gallery

A real cast-iron bench was used by Marisol in her amusing sculpture group at left. Marisol often represents herself in her works; in this group she is the child, holding up a cut-out steel umbrella for her mother. The bodies of the people are represented by boxlike shapes of steel; the faces, legs, hands and feet are molded of bronze.

While digging a garden, Richard Stankiewicz came upon a pile of old scrap metal. He decided to form sculpture that represents our machine civilization out of material that is considered "junk." From parts of discarded household appliances, pots and pans, automobiles or bicycles, Stankiewicz creates figures that seem about to move. *Kabuki Dancer* is his name for the creation at far right.

Richard Kienholz's *Friendly Grey Computer, Star Gauge Model #54* really does move. It rocks, rings, lights up and even answers questions. The artist used actual things, including a telephone and legs from an old doll, to make his construction. Kienholz, who lives in California, is a skilled carpenter, metalsmith and electrician. The artist's tools in his studio include hammers, power saws and chisels.

1956, cast iron and steel,
Whitney Museum of American Art,
Gift of the Friends of
Whitney Museum of American Art

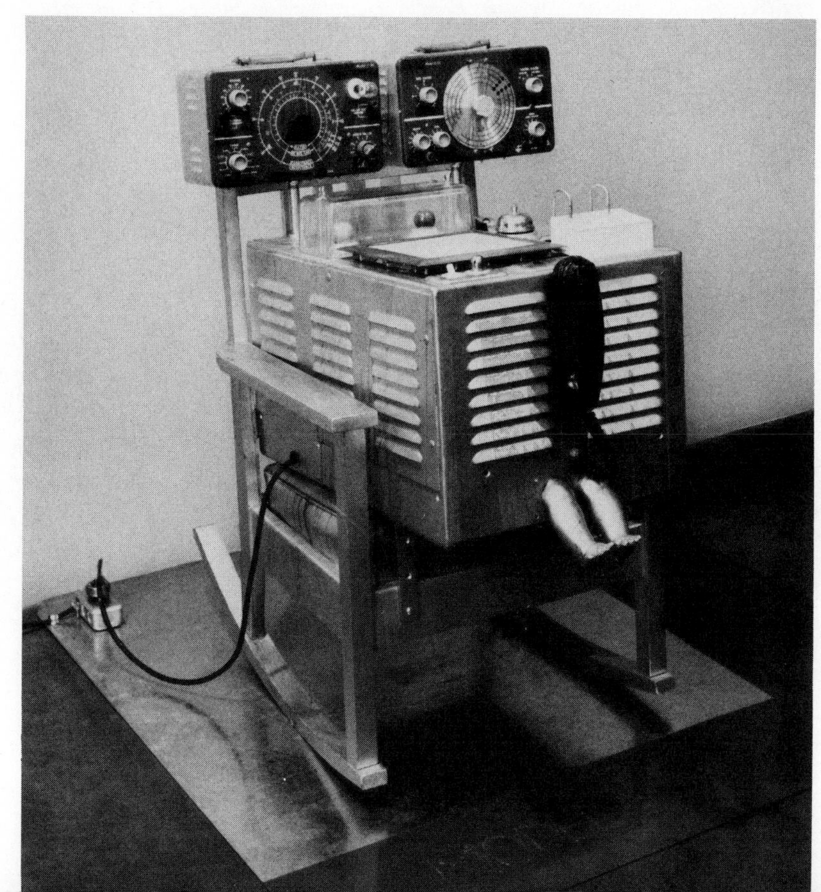

1965, Museum of
Modern Art, Gift of
Jean and Howard Lipman

1974, painted masonite and plywood, courtesy Leo Castelli Ga

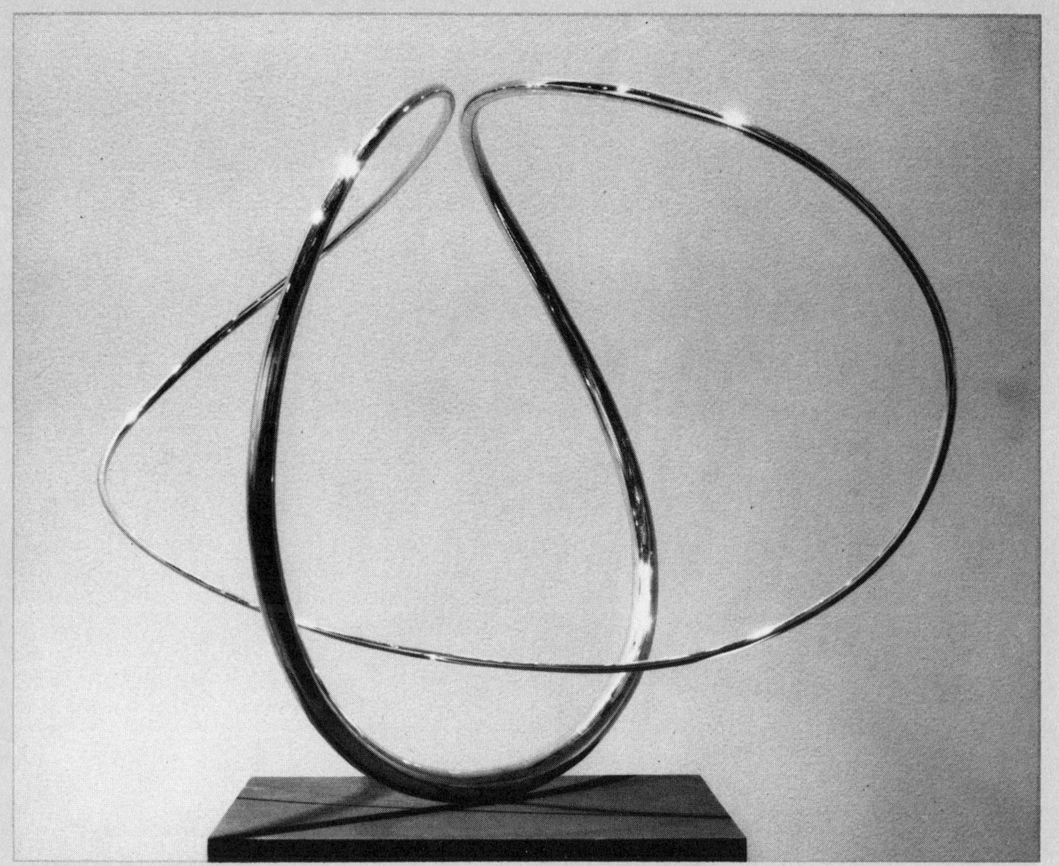

Construction #93, 1966, bronze, Collection of Mr. and Mrs. Philip M. Stern, courtesy Grace Borgenicht Gallery, New York

Robert Morris's idea is to involve art with life. The audience participates in *Labyrinth,* a structure thirty feet wide and eight feet high, made from thin boards and painted. People can walk through the narrow corridors, looking at the work from different positions. Morris sometimes makes sculptures of perfectly simple boxes and from soft felt cloth. He also makes "earthworks," oddly shaped piles of earth which have to be broken up when they are removed after an exhibition.

A turntable driven by a motor rotates José de Rivera's abstract sculpture above. It is made of rods of metal that have been forged, or shaped by heating and hammering. As it moves, light is reflected from different surfaces of the polished metal. Sculpture that moves is called "kinetic sculpture."

Aluminum that has been cut into a variety of shapes and welded together, then painted black, forms *Forest V* by Louise Nevelson at right. Nevelson is well known for her wall-size constructions made up of compartments and boxes fitted together and filled with objects she has found.

In the years since World War II, American artists have experimented with almost every known material, natural or man-made, and have developed exciting new approaches to painting and sculpture.

American painting and sculpture began, in colonial times, as a part of European art. Over the years, styles of art changed with the changing lives of the people. Now, three hundred years later, the freshness, freedom and energy of American artists have made the United States the art center of the world.

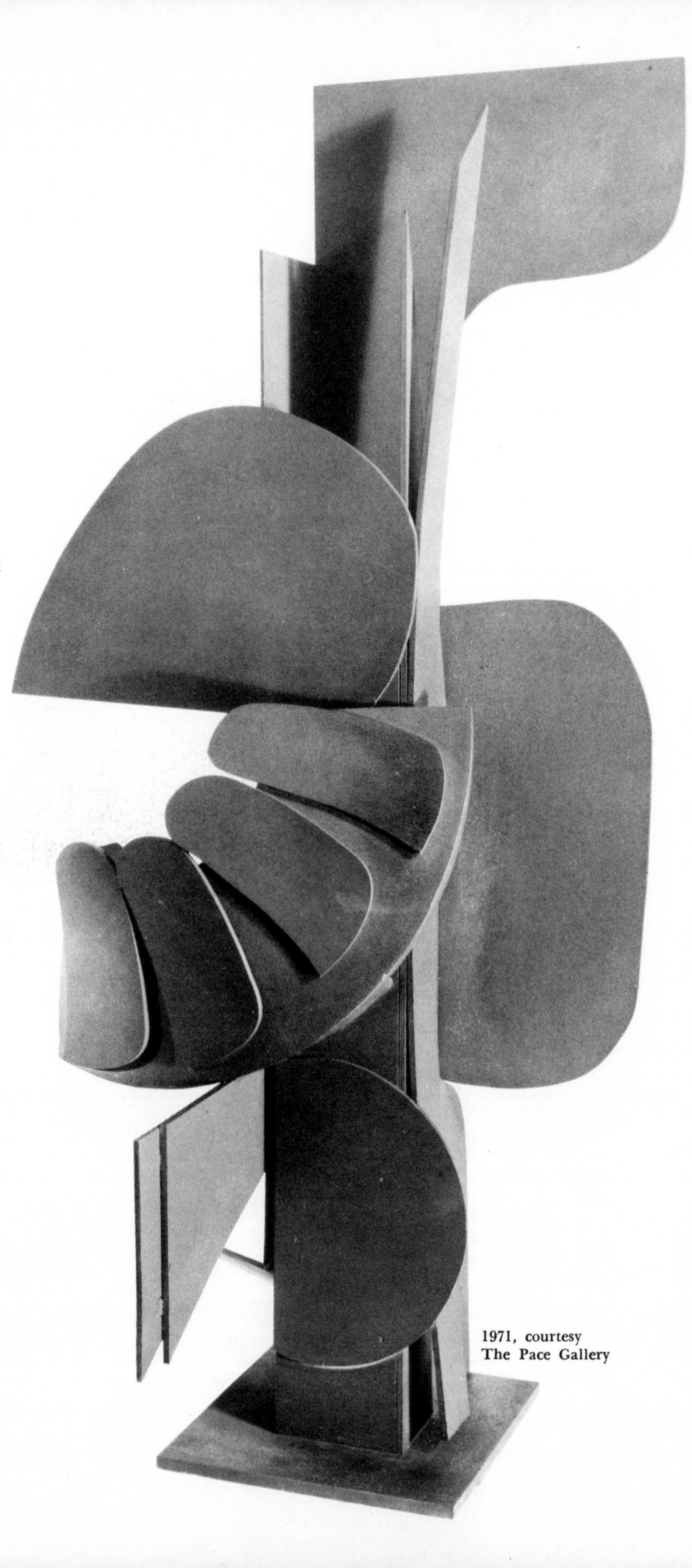

1971, courtesy
The Pace Gallery

Campbell's
CONDENSED
MINESTRONE
SOUP

Campbell's
CONDENSED
CREAM OF VEGETABLE
SOUP

Campbell's
CONDENSED
TURKEY
NOODLE
SOUP

Campbell's
CONDENSED
PEPPER POT
SOUP

Campbell's
CONDENSED
CONSOMMÉ
(BEEF)
SOUP

Campbell's
CONDENSED
CLAM CHOWDER
SOUP

Campbell's
CONDENSED
BLACK BEAN
SOUP

Campbell's
CONDENSED
CHICKEN
VEGETABLE
SOUP

Campbell's
CONDENSED
BEEF BROTH
(BOUILLON)
SOUP

Campbell's
CONDENSED
BEEF
SOUP

Campbell's
CONDENSED
CREAM OF
ASPARAGUS
SOUP

Campbell's
CONDENSED
VEGETARIAN
VEGETABLE
SOUP

Campbell's
CONDENSED
CHICKEN
WITH RICE
SOUP

Campbell's
CONDENSED
VEGETABLE
BEAN
SOUP

Campbell's
CONDENSED
CREAM OF
CELERY
SOUP

Campbell's
CONDENSED
CHICKEN
GUMBO
SOUP

Campbell's
CONDENSED
BEAN
WITH BACON
SOUP

Campbell's
CONDENSED
CHICKEN
NOODLE
SOUP

Campbell's
CONDENSED
VEGETABLE
SOUP

Campbell's
CONDENSED
TOMATO
SOUP